Monkey Lightning

MONKEY LIGHTNING

martha zweig

MONKEY LIGHTNING

TUPELO PRESS
NORTH ADAMS, MASSACHUSETTS

Library of Congress Cataloging-in-Publication Data
Zweig, Martha.
Monkey lightning : poems / Martha Zweig. — 1st pbk. ed.
p. cm.
ISBN-13: 978-1-932195-82-8 (pbk. : alk. paper)
ISBN-10: 1-932195-82-3 (pbk. : alk. paper)
I. Title.
PS3576.W37M66 2010
811'.54—dc22

2009043985

Cover and text designed by William Kuch of WK Graphic Design.

Printed in the United States by BookMobile on FSC-certified recycled paper,
with electricity from wind energy.

First paperback edition February 2010.
13 12 11 10   5 4 3 2

Tupelo Press
P.O. Box 1767, North Adams, Massachusetts 01247
Telephone: (413) 664–9611 / Fax: (413) 664–9711
editor@tupelopress.org / www.tupelopress.org

Tupelo Press is an award-winning independent literary press that publishes fine
fiction, non-fiction, and poetry in books that are a joy to hold as well as read.
Tupelo Press is a registered 501(c)3 non-profit organization, and we rely on public
support to carry out our mission of publishing extraordinary work that may be
outside the realm of the large commercial publishers. Financial donations are
welcome and are tax deductible.

Supported in part by an award from
the National Endowment for the Arts

NATIONAL
ENDOWMENT
FOR THE ARTS

CONTENTS

—*1*—

INVOCATION

So perched the preying
mantis as if to beg pardon:
I have always lived in a little grass shack.
It doesn't take an everlovin' blue-eyed
hurricane to witness God's
will leaving you for dead wrong, either.
Yet I love you still,

my shamelessly unreliable, I
pick you again for the sheer mind.
Even admit it: I did betray the slightest
emotion. Sad day to have come to, hint
of the heartfelt all chewed
over & spit for motes & beams, yet pluck
my ripe rows in the all-seeing eye's corner.

I like a slow season. Allow the thing
its sweetening heat, fruit-heart, the hush
it adjusts to, fostering seed.
With luck, gobbled up & dropped again
in fresh indignities of dung to prosper far
afield, prove autoerotic
enough to support my song.

HYPNAGOGIC

Thank you. I slept so comfortably that upon
awakening in a brief racket of the birds I slept
at once a second time, & so on. Human

beings lost their fur because the tongues they
could've used to pant with got themselves caught up
in language instead, hence naked & sweaty

chitchat & to this day, which I figured out
myself painting the porch in the sun with my love,
that excellent dry spell in July. Sleep

in vocables. The clouds come home, lumber in
their big white weeksworth of marketing from the ends
of the earth & with this surprise for me, a blue

gooseflesh I'm to climb into & zip the teeth
straight to my chin for when the Lord arrives, picks
you up dead by the scruff of your soul & you never

tug again at your bright morning thread. Your plot's dear
loose end! It withers, & little enough made of it in its
heyday, say, as a snake in the hollyhocks

oozing bees when the glamorous lady cried *Look,
look!* & it rustled & shined itself dragonwise
in & out along the vines to its best advantage.

Here's what the world's coming to, faint of heart &
benighted: a miniature of the eye in its tender
lid & flushed with tears even before it opens.

FACETIOUS

Pointless love makes the world flutter & shine.
Nobody keeps track which darling was whose:
don't begrudge yours, I didn't begrudge mine.

Participatory songbird! —a fine-
feathery musical air that pursues
pointless love makes the world flutter & shine.

First blush? Furious tears? One asinine
bellow? —negligible sting, a bee's news.
Don't begrudge yours, I didn't begrudge mine.

Implicate us & extricate, design
each resolves as the other misconstrues:
pointless love makes the world flutter & shine

as pond dimples disengage & combine
into mingling faces we trick & choose.
Don't begrudge yours, I didn't begrudge mine.

Six kisses left, of life? Blow five! —benign
dispensation somebody else can use:
don't begrudge yours, I didn't begrudge mine.
Pointless love makes the world flutter & shine.

THE TWO BOWLS

Of such small matter,
of the bumps & grinds
of water through motions,
sunshine merrymakes one of its
appearances & thins away:
rocky applause.

Any brook's a tease. What
of it what of it continue
the birds, & the vegetable world
sheds itself seed & clouds prowl
high aisles of the sky
to fill on hunger

& under them both my bowls tilt
to clap for some too, & round
& hollow themselves, pity, & there
rises light again from the soles
of my feet to the tops of my eyes
& brims with common pollens.

Given this gold dust,
& given it gives death
heartier doing than lust,
then your good night's
sleep is to wake at all at
all say the shades.

TOMATO ASPIC ELEGY

Charlotte Louise Etzold MacNeal, 1910–1989

It's where we stick those some things best
strictly left alone, deep in opaque
agglutination in, as it were, the primitive dinner-&-dancing-
party hostess brain. *Your mama dresses her & you*
up this spiffy, then she make her
best people eat that? O love-
apple, flesh the sun
starts on the vine, ripen to this:
what we can hack up we can choke down, thus —
dollop of mayonnaise, dazzle of good silver, the slightly
smeared lettuce leaf one leaves.

Time or two we girls played at elegant ladies,
sprinkled a pinch of magenta sand over our poor beach
sting jellies, each
individually embedded quatrefoil, & served
with a stick on frilliest kelp. Who'll thrill
any one of us grown women to any pure poison again
like that? The sea
that blubbers in the wrecks of empire will; the sea nibbles
already the slippers that mother swole up such a lickety pair
of feet in that she quickly kicked
us off behind the davenport.

To be sure, I'm the mere
spectacle of myself, she sighed at last, slid into hospice. *Sweet,*
do you know, whatever became of the nervous system I
so liked? People must think . . . Horselaughter, ma,
they'll owe you an entertainment, your infectious
gaiety shook in the very napery, put out your long

vigorous lips to me, goodbye, but like some dear dapple nag huff-
puffing along to the big black brick glue
factory where they boil up bones for their goo. Incorrigible
flirt that she still was, she went snappy-hipped &
swayback the whole way.

LAPIS

Perry Scott MacNeal, 1913–1997

Lapins lazuli; blue bunnies, bluebonnets, lazily
Lazarus unwinds his sheets to the breeze,
to the Maypole girls. Maples match him, banner
to stinking shred. It's spring & literalminded Jesus'
trick has horrified the company.
Godforbid any such transgression again!

But let these twenty pastel minxes circulate &
plait their ribbons round the wretched man.
He was the Good Shepherd's crony. Coneys,
immigrant bunnies, once overran an
unimportant New World island, now whose amusement
park deteriorates by creaks & groans, even as Good

Shepherdess Bo-Peep, cherishing an idle crook, perfects
benign neglect: her charges also lost animals.
Our own young ladies weeks ago doffed azure Easter
millinery & settled down to plot Memorial
Day's parade, but here staggers-ever-onwards Lazarus,
grisly enough to distress any military festivity—

he belongs in a hole in the ground
(mammal burrow, huddled up with the babies).

WE MAY ALL KNOW

Fishes as well have deaths.
In the lake shallows scores
of alewives bob, bent sideways;
quarter-inch fur of rot, cocoon
all over works each inside out.

They suffer their deaths unblinking,
roll up on the beach and drain.
Whisks of the sand, sun and air
dry their bodies out crisp, light
now, papery as festival kites.

Plainly less various than the kinds
of life, dying must be also
birdlike and flowerlike
and what we may all know
of all, even the unicellular,

decay track and blip in the cloud chamber,
nothing no creature ignorant or overlooked.

GREEN VELVET

Shallows: kayak bobs me to drowse like Moses,
river-foundling. Curtsy & skim me, cordial
reeds. Divert a princess to bare her feet to
splash in & grab me!

★

Cushy sinecure, the composer lily-
paddles note-to-note on her staff. Her turban
snags & launches damselflies: tip my finger,
flick off to founder.

★

Gown milady's seamstress devised of twenty-
seven thousand senseless male mallard heads has
left the lake unthinkable, vapid; drags her
hips in its torpor.

★

Interregnum. Mildew corrupts the palace.
Blabbermouths collaborate; latterday-&-
dark they flap & yackety-yak behind an
overrun garden.

★

Centuries-to-let: our descendants swap &
furnish makeshift terraces, north wing, south wing.
Plush-upholstered boulders indulge the fog that
sifts in the cedars.

BUBBLEBATH

Suggestively it purports to hide the busy
bodies in movies: what do you suppose those
two are up to, grappling in there? Then the one sinks
& the other lifts up & steps out clattering
a razor & the froth turns pink. From an unseen
front door, street noise & the next woman's voice: briskly
she lets herself in, calls out, "Heighdy, darling! . . ." —*o*
please, hey, just a minute there, is that you?

Trafficky ocean serves up a foam, skim
of sailors & treasure, ancient losses, the botch-broth
of ruling nations, queen-spittle. Queen must drag the severe
salt in her own laundry now, even as her impotent liege
fulminates like all the clouds of heaven locked
in a single crown. Centuries past & to seethe so over
the wrack & ruin still! Their ships breach & roll: toil, war, toil;
breezes skip the spume in fluffy clots along the shingle.

A creature, the mindless slug, will bubble to death
in a sprinkle of salt, children. Upon your mother's
crimson rainy rose, observe, thus: little bunch just
fizzes up all suds, thrashing. Some powers that rise
only indifferently after a while to the normal
adult occasion may altogether recharge
to such a spectacle. Surprises abound this world!
Who knows how, now? What useful art to make of it?

CHAGRIN

Heinously wronged again,
why would my victim stoop to a squeak of mine, my remorse?

How to contrive
upon my shame some more-than-mere
formality to exemplify how sorry I am?
— following in my footwork a regress of repulsive
shoes to drag one
behind another, shriveling
their laces!
                or decent Mistress Gardenia visits
my cheek with her tarnish the smutch
of quicksilver, & my blush defects from what little nerve.

Under the circumstances, the worm.

O the lugubrious
bony birds will hardly prey
on me, but they flinch their
nostrils in aversion;

my fingerprints
recoil, even my dust
pirouettes to inquire
elsewhere, offers itself to rise in my detractors' bread.

Or shall I crumple into the lost luggage where someone
else's soiled sleeve
& hem may cover me?

The buttonholes. A polite cough.

AWAY/HOME

for Marion French

Awful bad girl I was, authorities whisked me away.
Incognito: bone-meanness froze what face I had awry,
& the name they filed me by instantly forged itself an airy
dismissal, nothing to it. O sniff me, buzz me high-wiry,
nerved up: nick a socket, firefangle the razor wire
& finger the ringling & brotherly circuits, flop me, tire
me to death, but luckily I fizzled at ancient-before-my-time.
I got old. Tucked into this hairnet & nuzzled up as gentle, tame
& meek as you-know. Me, reportedly. Or one-&-the-same.
Pleased to acquaint you, I spoke up now-&-then-some:
ain't-broke a don't-fixed grin, prinked along ladylike, went home.

MEMENTO MORI

I am so fat that my whole body gets in my way.
"Will you just quit crowding me!" I yell. *I will
soon enough,* it replies, *only not quite yet.*

I must pry my little wristwatch out of a deepening
flesh crevice to get what time, but my body explains it is making
the most of itself ere we turn up seriously late.

I wanted a bath: no room in the tub today for the water.
No womb! exults the body. *Forget it! Get born! Grow up!*
& by way of repeated illustration, grows.

I miss my daily walk. "Who's seen shoes or my feet?" I call.
Silence: nobody miles around to find me. Never mind— the part
behind the scenery can still rehearse, trembling so in wings—

alas! I must drop the next amazing costume upon the last.
Eying each one against me, the body advises: *Put it by. The essential
garment will fit more dreadfully, even without size.*

QUINTESSA

As full-bloom of the whale is its blubber
& musically the whole whale thrums & keens,
& as whale wit itself smarts deep in the core
of the buoyant tonnage of its tremendous bodying-forth,
so the Fat Lady who sings *the end*

the end is near fetches her warble, too, from the quick—
shiftily in her tipsy balances offsets
the extravagant yaw of her lipids against the soul
that a mellow note may squeeze the more readily,
happily upwards to shimmy forth.

Later her lover plucks in her armpit —insistently pungent
& hairy in damply matted copious coils—; he twiddles
a knot there, works it, unravels it out & along
the near one of her whoppingly artlessly sideswiped
mammaries to pique the ticklish

nipple as singular & eminent upon its rise
as any mountain summit's cairn that every pilgrim lo
these many years has put the one more token
local stone to— croons to her, teases the not-quite-
malignant-yet flesh there to tip up one more cell.

COUNTER-FABLE

Dear preposterous
grasshopper of opposite-
angled knees, glitch, insistent screed
of disproportionate bliss, I put my trust
in domestic economy once, eschewed
excess of appetite & disrepute, kicked the likes-of-
you con-over-career—

I recant. Field pillagers, who conspicuously
overrun the locale, welcome! — infest my circumspect
securities & exchange, day-in-day-out
pester askew the topiary hedges. Offertory: I
resign my estate. Do I quibble some? then shrilly
buzzknuckles-&-shins
dismember & remind me.

What hideous best bug
face any one of you puts on & tilts
to fool me, will. Fill
of folly I laid up long ago exhales: stale
meadowy breath exhuming out of the crib & dry
disintegrating bales, savory yet of the odd blossom,
grass sex, inimical thistle. Choked down

mostly what exhaustible bowl of dust I get, is why I
crave more, why scrape the floor, next attic
shelves, hurl spinning
hats into the shoe trees. Strum cheek-
by-my-jowl any green musician at all! — instigate in my crawl
spaces fiendish undoings, strip my stewardly
jacket & leggings for tatters & wings.

COHABITATION: MIND AND BODY

There's no sense
in settling down on the body's terms.
Finally it will turn you out.

It comes to no matter
in the end that you have fed it,
warmed it, served its peculiar whims

all this time;
it grows balky and snappish,
will not be moved by any

appeal to occasions
of better sympathy. There's a fatal
ruin in the arrangement.

Still, every
mother's daughter knows there's a fine
hum on the skin in season,

and one can't
go against nature forever.
In any case, it involves only

that imminence of heartbreak
on which a certain kind
of love thrives.

PUNCTUAL

Springtime in the apple trees, boing boing twig
blossom to twig the bumblebee goes, but I put up with more than a little
too much sweetness already from last fall. Yuck, love!

By a spongy light edging around the globe the twentieth
century's horrid age spots willy-nilly effloresce. My homesickly
bedfellow must belong to some lost other hundred years

I pricked my finger & both of us slept through: blot
of my blood-dropt index tip clotted a stitch in the orchard-
colored flounce. Rumples itself about to embody us &

surprise! —we're tedious. Nurse Grudge, are you there?
Is he dead? Have I got the no-good-reason all to myself,
foremost of later-in-life's beatific resuscitudes?

But she props up a steamy tray, & he rolls over & slops the broth, chip
my saucer. He cheats at toast, I remember; glowers
down weather. Once when I meant what I said I swore off

a smart-aleck remark, then *better days are coming*
murmured a dulcet tone. But I didn't care for the better
days much either, did I, dearest? or for long.

MIDSUMMER MARITAL WITH CREOSOTE BUSH
& TATTOO

Can't expect too much of a person. Little or no
telling why. Well enough, left alone,
tends to wander off into that scapegoat's
aura who staggers around the desert's
volatile prospects in & out of the shapes— two-thirds
of them feminine— of sin, & snatches at dry
shrubs & prickers, bleats among bleating husks.
Things' shadows rise up inflammatory.

Don't be a churl, darling. It's too hot today to live
any more or less. Over-bothered already
to put in an appearance. Freak of humidity,
vapor off of that ruminant out there,
consorts with mordant spirits to visit our
bodies' pits. Synopsis: eight prognostic instances & each
one's opposite swelter in the mirage. Rub me out? —but I'd just
as soon cooperate, strip, blot into your oily rag

as not. Adore me or not as the dead giveaway steals
about the facial features. Or stop me once you've never
heard the end of our point-by-point
reconciliation: all-but-certain atrophy. The sweat's
in the subcutaneous text. Ultraviolet limns the script's
initials as ornamental beasts until I look illegible
even in my own words, & then whatever they say you concur.
What passes for time around here, I'm telling you.

FEATHERED FRIENDS

On Spectacle Pond a laggard loon yelped, next
I saw it, next I didn't. Hardly mannerly
of me to paddle out chasing the loons, but I did.

High fall color, but leaves upon leaves,
spotty this year, begrudge themselves. They remind
me of me, trying on grade school dresses in ill will.

Undone! Obstinate spirit undoing! —reiterates
whatchamacallit, territorial chirp of the backwater nondescript.
Every so often my heart sinks without a trace.

Shaggy pond, in finite patience, means to shrink itself
soon to a meadow: tree-by-toppling-over-
tree it raddles its rough edges gradually inwards.

Despised exotic once myself, I did my stint of fish-&-wildlife
mischief & thrived. (Among profuse apologies a few
fresh aspersions cast, with luck nobody gets them.)

Most maple leaves alight face-down. Buoyant on tips
on the facile surface, they round their silvery
wrongsides up & erect red stems; swanlike, disperse.

Brief breather, then parties to refractory
local hostilities resume: in a twinkling I snap up a modest
rocky lakefront property, post my dissuasion.

The pond mistakes itself for the time being.
Inevitably most pond creatures fall prey.
The pond quibbles and turns to itself a deaf ear.

Solicitudes, regrets: community civilities
too proliferate upon so little to recommend them that I do
relish a tongue-lashing followed by laughter.

Subject to lunatic humors, myopic of eye & woozy,
I poured myself some glasses of water. Binocular
blink: those two look to me like the same pair, year after year.

REVERBERANT

Near bank off to the farthest marsh & back again across
Bucknaked Lake, leisurely, with paper bag
of apricots: O golden hind-
ends, buttock-niceties I nip
& sneak a quick read
ahead in my unexpectedly fiendish
pageturner as the rowboat slips,

I've dribbled on paragraphs & lost what little place
I had. I thought we were bound & determined, but no,
prodigies intrude
among the unstable characters & seem to have seized impending
developments & run off with some other & irresistible
narrative fan into the glitzy apartments of light,
leaving me to my devices.

I adore even your loose pits, kiss-&-toss.
Summary plot: the heroine's flesh eats. Minnows I never
quite follow nudge concrete crumbs off the sunken municipal
monument, whose vandals stepped-right-up
into divine wings just as the reverend raven
shrieked they would above the overwrought & trashy sand,
somebody's popcorn— I wasn't there, but I heard. The toughest act

to follow, somebody sang, is of love. Two for instance
hobgoblets of wine tablehopping your picnic may rap up
a paramourous seance: hand-in-hand your intimate
circle since carnal history's earliest
incident may agitate at once & globally, blush each
to each affected organ— so it strikes me, & tipsy
still in my innermost ear, after an argument from design.

SENTIMENTAL

Dummy, you know you know
better than to stoop into your own
dark car like that & start.
Asking for it!
Maybe you even perform
astutely enough the entire
repertoire of resistance
at your command,
but there you've got that country-
&-Western song
still crawling out of the radio:

you didn't, don't
ever hit the button in time,
so of course & by brutest
assault it yanks you clean
off the highway, strips
you of irony & thrusts
in in a moment, unrapes
you & dumps you as-it-were
virgin there, in the briars, in tears.

UROGENITAL

Everything I know I learned from the dirty parts.
Itch, seeped the organs, a giggle.
Convulsed among themselves: We're a mammal.
Pushing urge! For fun one bulged at another.

Dirty bicycle lurched the curb, dirty egg basket, & never
more insinuatingly so than when you pick &
choose like that among a few innocent errands, you nasty
slug, you, mother's hydrangea fumed.
Spoke up her caterpillar, that's not either
your periwinkle, it belongs to God
(landlady adjacent, who kept the fierce, indignant dog).
Blurted a hydrant, into the gutter, missy, there's where some a tiny
bit less fortunate wouldn't turn up their nose.

Ventriloquist, get your hand out of my jaw.
Get your arm down out of my gown. What words
didn't I twist! —mother protested, mostly her own
sweet ones & worse,
mostly her deckled letters, "Dear
dead days beyond recall," sheets of her purple
cursive that gushed & kissed at my fingers in passing, & clanged
shut & descended
by loops battily down the incinerator to hell

so that nowadays, every time I throw up & flip
the john lever to flush,
her *goodness gracious!* still sloshes around my pink ear.

Licensed professional? you wish! —abreast
of pertinent expertise & packing cutting-edge
gadgets to plunge
your impacted traps & disinfect your drains?
Sanitary in any sex? —buzz me, I might be your girl.

GETTING AWAY

You see touch too
has convinced her otherwise:

no more than if you twisted grass
into the other grass to keep the ocean
or nudged all the nearby stones to a fit
while birds landed and birds left
setting their feet down   tucking their feet up
and evening collected the whole meadow around
like a big finished picnic
expect her,

sexual hands,
drovers of the herds of the body.
She's not there.

How they hate to be roused for this!
When they give up and switch the flashlights
off they snap the white beams like her
wrists if they could just get her back.

INDICATIVE

Might as well try to punish the sea
for running off repeatedly with lo! ye gods
& little fishes, or try to upbraid it home two hours
early among the giddy reefs again, as complain
now because I seem to have spoiled my appetites
on nothing but a burst bag of salt
brittle left of the surf.

Bit sick to the stomach. High & dry the same
bottled note probably still says (as bottled
notes frequently pitch a passing breeze to do): *the vessel*
wallowed, crew lost heart, never mind. No stranger
myself, but slosh in to-&-fro my worthless
valuables & cower & scrub until it comes over me:
superstitious ingenuity, I've half a notion.

Woman on the beach, whom I meanwhile nipped the end
of my umbilical thread & gave it to, lips it & tricks
it straight into her needle's one conniving
wink. All afternoon she stitches
the sand in her lap. "Once I finish up
this placket," she says, "it will be almost time.
Not quite time, but it will do for now."

GHAZAL: INTERVALS

High flood turns, gradually drains off to the dead slack of time.
Another desert blows over another lost track of time.

When she wants to stay lost, her own mother's vibrant nerves sputter,
catch nothing but the faint twinge, hint, flicker, whiff and smack of time.

When she wants to get found, long backslashes of ocean rear up,
overturn, slosh her slight ruins up along the wrack of time.

Nighttime: groupers and angels sleep in the reef; crustaceans walk.
Or she and lively lizards dart across the forked crack of time.

Poor sunken ships! deaf gone dumb to the humpbacks' consultation.
Canyon rim— listen: wolfish Alpha howls in the pack of time.

Face to what face, who inhabits these colossal kelp forests?
Or a campfire sparks the battered moon, blue of and black of time.

To this day, as glaciers drop fresh calves into the knocking sea,
cubs try the incisive sabertoothed snicker and snack of time.

No uproar hurries her, salt gale or sandstorm mounted upwind—
maybe her burro licked up the last lingering lack of time.

Porpoise to wildebeest, no mother taught her those two tokens,
tick and tock, or tucked her in against any attack of time.

Fancy eye, the crow picks over her dust patch for curios,
pecks at glints nimbly switching glints in the nick and knack of time.

Trickster Martha, she who sometimes parches to death, or else drowns:
bounced out the front, she ducks around, back in at the back of time.

RESURGENT

All night sleep towards the thunder, & then,
as a last dud of it croaks off dully away
behind Buffalo Mountain's hump, it occurs
to you you could try to wake up, but you don't.

Snakehips the river bumps under the house
& will dribble the sills & chuck the cellar
shelves down, dozen dusty jelly jars
drop like so many stones, humblest & handy

stones that anyone picks to tie in a robe & swirl
far enough out to feed yourself to the fishes,
scoop fishes alive into the sleeves & slippers where elbow-
& ankle-bone stood patiently waiting their turns

to knock now in the congregation of waters,
sing in the key of oarlocks engaging for someone
to drag the loops of the rain but just miss you, the note
of one hinge, that one-or-another occasion flood

pried the gate back resistant years & the dog
churned by with foaming stumps & furniture, & the more
stoutly paddled in peril than help though relations
yelled you your loudest name off the bobbing porch—

Bluetick tonight circles a bed of its own in yours the three times
it takes to unsettle. Hollow sister in a damp sheet takes up
almost all the air, hisses with it how insufferably
simplemindedly you rise, again, daily, to risen light.

VERONICA

Strange neighborhood, clear dotty
night sprigged with stars: immediately I took after
one man into deep greed.
He plays the forks, rakes, stricken tines.

I realized my knees rustling
his fringe caused an additional (faint) noise. And before
I got too accustomed I sang
supper, laid linen over the planks & sawhorses, wrung

my hands, trickled kitchen soup. O gratitude
he does not cry, neither do I.

Brass note cranks in the pipes in another
building, crosstown;
distinct water garble— not in this life.
                                        We sip
gold flecks kiss by kiss
against the birdy sill. I dabble
his salty face as he sniffs
my neck feathers & wrist smidgens, & nibbles
the phosphorescent napkin rings raw.

CHATTER

You'll hear it: adamantly
the dead still scratch for time &
get none. But this is
Tuesday sunshine on your own
live knucklebones;
fingerprinted window,
all it takes is
opening—
   the sapling
birches in commotion dip
to act the necessary
simpletons conducting company,
fitted out in modest time &
ostentatious time as
skull bells, clear globes of lit
air, shy
droplets tingling for somebody, you,
to take,
  & if you do you
may match instantaneous
mind to mind the chickadees
who speechify each
other & the waters.

HYSTERIA

Gurgle out beyond the yellow willow pricks a twinge
in your nipples: you thought, ah! baby
in the bulrushes! & hurried over, but it was that
bad little fox talked jabber & dribbled,
& now you stagger
out gifted, bitten woman, like gotten
religion, upper lip a blood blister,
stumblebum, nervy, & dangerous.

Bitches to dogs wriggle up a posture just like
this one to the Angel! & she demonstrates.
Morning she hung wet linen swollen
with sunshine & soon girls flapped amok in it,
yanked sheets & screeched; she clapped
two hymns together & testified these juicy
teeth pour the divine virus, your own mothers
remember, darlings, she divulges: urges us, ask!

Toss her, hobble her, even report she
managed to grunt at us to church her good
& proper the one more time, robed
red & choir-pewed, begged us grin
& hear out her spittle from a knock-
knock-who's joke stuck in her giggly
throat through to the final hiccups & vixen-
rictus dregs of glossolalia.

MISTRESS HERE

Old underbitch gets a
biscuit, yah my new tricks
rivet the kids, as if a
God granted prayers, a
pony instantly bedside, the
bully next door burst into flames.
They adore me & tug me
quick upstairs to their inscrutable rooms.
Thus does my tenure already
turn to the good. It keeps a
wife pleased as well below at her stitch,
a motto coming along into its own
curly letters entwined. What a
flourish of charities begins
at this home in her name! She will
kiss & primp them & bustle each abroad.

On the contrary,
not the half of it;
hand over quaint hand old
mother-smitten invisible
sister help haul the buckets up of our
heart blinking cheeky frogs: I'm
paying you for it in real children.

2

INTRODUCTORY

For tonight we've invited a live
potato to speak. Please welcome the potato.
Elsie, over there, assisting, who also
has spread herself wide for somebody's butter
& fork & says she has not liked it,
will screen your written questions for redundance,
relevance, & courtesy. Pass them on in after.

Famine, then! —a staple poor people
cultivate less worldwide, we hope, than formerly,
may remind many in this
audience of the potato. The history
of vegetables, like that of animals & minerals,
rides multiple raggedy waves into our own,
boggling upon prosperity. How does our uniquely

qualified authority elaborate the point? Intent
curiosity attends potatoes' every appearance:
we've fretted ourselves over what underground
they prepare. Can we take a particular potato,
becomingly scrubbed, as you see,
reliably to represent the basic comestibles
in variety, rice, say; manioc, the kernels, countless beans?

But enough! —programs shuffling! Undeservedly
& twice favored this evening, we acknowledge it's
taken your committee quite some doing.
Eyes gouged out, even boiled in oil, potatoes
rarely confess & never give names, except,
this once, suggested Elsie's, who, the very moment
we approached her, volunteered.

THE HIGHEST STANDARD OF LIVING IN THE WORLD

Rabbit out of a
hat don't tell
you any truth, it
just hangs there from its
grabbed ears kicking,

meanwhile that's your
boss
bowing & grinning in
tie & tails &
silk scarves flying out of midair, you

perfectly well
know this trick by
heart all week & overtime, so

what we got is
not like poof! but
gonna make him really disappear

OUT

You'll go,
kicking &
screaming, oh
yes you'll go
because
it's time, the frost
in the gutter dazzles you at
sunrise, you
won't put off another day;

no ordinary
death jimmies the
window from there to
here like
this, with such
furious noise &
wild signals looking for a
little more help
from the inside, it's

bright ice a knife a
sliver a gun & a fine
cold morning harangue, if
you still scare easy the
drawers just dump your
things the
bed strips the
decent room evacuates
off you go

GHAZAL Y2K

Weather channel sublimes women into thin air.
Cold snap: reports men & children into thin air.

When they took the magician (apart) at her word,
sleeves tucked her inside out again, into thin air.

Defenestrate the philodendron, my assets!
—commingled, movered-and-shaken into thin air.

Sweatshoppes fully involved, rumor mills squeal alarm:
fire crew scrambled up the siren into thin air.

Artifice scans documents, spots regulations,
eyes the natural citizen into thin air.

True-false, multiple choice, fill-in-the-blank, pause here:
the next three questions open into thin air.

Huff puffed up the creature-featured speaker balloon:
—expansive pink grimace swollen into thin air.

Fuss & flap & sooner than later the sky falls:
feather dust lofts Little Chicken into thin air.

No wonder your life suddenly turns meaningless!
—sins forgiven & forgotten into thin air.

Martha? Who? Not here. Did she follow directions?
One of those sadly mistaken into thin air.

BRAINWASH

To be sure, those civilizations
that dicker novelties, notions, along
my original impulse would swoop
around to appear to my eyes
infinitesimally small
if they could, but they are too small. Even the vast
galactic regions they mount successions
of empires to overrun, with the light-years
seeping between them, are too small.

Intelligence charters their colonies to wink
& dwindle alone. Limb of the universe
almost never stirs, numb, infected with god.
They rake little skies
with mathematics & hurl
their crockery into what light
reaches them & play
crackpot hunches deep in provisional governments
where the counterintuitive laws pass.

Not since the human fontanel I kissed
once have I wished
anyone well or anyone's enemies
ill, ill. I haven't cared if the stroke
of doom. I justify myself: a signal
switch set, a rigged trinket, their ship apart,
their vanishing act, a vandal, puff of the hordes,
the no idea ever to cross their
minds unbidden, seamless arctic.

INCARNATION

Nothing can happen unbecoming
their dispositions: from water to mud to
air in a twinkling they change, and whirl from
their bristling bones like snow; like sparks they jump
immense gaps, but they all have to be driven

through slaughter because they will not go
except bucking and snapping the whole way.
See, they have turned as merciless as moons
because they do not love time their bodies
are taken to tell, and clench them and their minds.

Wherever worlds and worlds' creatures are,
and not nothing, make them curious to
understand; make them open their mouths and
stems and stones, selfsame flesh that a word
at once renders to motion through once again.

WITNESSES

All around the villagers swirls
a swimmer's disturbance,
resolves them rolled in
vectors like thinnest chains,
arrays them in age
of their bodies' each-
&-every quick-change.

They will testify, "We admire
the fluency of this cloth,
all it can divulge.
But when the flesh wears off
our own love and hate
for good, that is no
miracle for us to praise."

In the shallows, light
laps a young coelacanth.
Time breeds and buoys
the fish, the people working; nets slap
and spread, like nerves catch at
this one, that one.
Busily one dies.

AGLEY

after Robert Burns

Harm not a hair
on your head of the god that
bit you. And as for that
we'll see about that, fear no
threatful muttering under
the weather, either.
Put no one to shame.
Speak to the frantic worms that deface
your brother,
calm them.

This is a voice speaking.
Your prettiest plan knows better in its
bones & so resists carrying-out,
like hefty trash. Reconsider
me, please. Before long
lengthens in passing past
all understanding, take this opportunity:
blue beard, red riding hood, green-
and-yellow basket: spare me
the gray area.

Police? Me? But I'm the glitch
from the stitch in time,
proverbial sidekick, savior of nine
for our mutual amusement, dabbler the wan
arts flap to for crusts. Oil-
of-warrior spreads on the troublesome
buoyant breasts; attar throbs
warmly at the pulse-points a woman
imitates who briefly thought
she'd sing one for you.

PALAVER

I've caught up to you too late, alas
I could save my breath. That one butterfly
especially tricks out & festoons;
the brook fusses along in tatty
frills & to what end? O none.
It will have its interminable
say on the first fair point you
venture towards a next until it has
lost your mind & exhausted nothing
whatsoever of all promise.
Don't interrupt me babbling either.
This one isn't about death.

Light insinuates from behind to
superimpose our own
shallows on these, & the three
swishy fishes you think you
see move in to inhabit your
shade flick into eight directions out.
Just so needles proliferate all
fancywork & to the naked eye it
looks like love. What got into you? A
water in the ear, smattering of the
tongues holyrollers speak in & the
upstart vainglories in full bloom!

THE PARTICULARS

A shell drops as in water.
When it opens, these are our bodies:
some green plants, some animals,
some machines, the stuffs and objects.

They are all moving at once.
They have their noises.
Who decides the nature of one
decides every other.

When they are studied they simplify,
all into the same fluid.
They mate in secret.
Anything can be born.

ZODIAC

1.

Resplendent cage, this star crate
slides up its cold white
slats for the night around me.
The soul is inside.
Slide up and click locked.

2.

From within
eyes blink out.
They are our eyes
in a latticed summerhouse.
Their black centers
contain constellations,
drawn lines of the light years.

3.

Rays of the stars
are all in place.
From here the criss cross
cat's cradle
slackens; then
pulls through a new figure.

4.

Believing it is in
its crib an infant
gropes fingers at the bars
the beams and is
instantly riddled with light.

ST. JOHN'S HEAD, HOY, ORKNEY ISLANDS

Clouds

Webster always starts it.
Webster slyly sends over her cats
to steal the breath from Spinster's
fat blotchy baby, so Spinster
catches at the cats' names & draws
the long cursive threads out— hence whole
societies of these vague loose
windbags in the sky: sulky
sad sacks, the disembodied.

Susceptible

Clean up your house, old wife! but yet-
to-come evening & already faint
fabrications hint anew in the curtains.
A headache suggests itself. Clumsy common
null, you— even the good staunch
furniture droops off just
slightly & will succumb. You need
someone to perform the lightest effleurage,
brush a buttercup by each eyelid.

Surrender

Good girl, I'm asleep. Is it much to ask
the preposterous weathers off the scarps
& around the pits to make peace?
But I never mind: my sheet
fills with lies & spreads wide its weave
& my sinuses seep with dream,
until come a here-kitty-
kitty & I lisp to the dear
little nostrils, shrivel me.

ATMOSPHERICS

Weather tucks in from the west.
Aspect of the future more
or less as forecast most
places along its way, it returns
from around the world.
Let us take in
what cosmopolitan airs arrive.
Let us take & contribute breath.

Seams & joints conforming, your own
house shuts the foul of weathers out,
admits the fair. But a house mortally
rides, too, upon more novel prospects:
bids, sales; certain clauses that trigger provisions that next
moment you find you've got no
say whatsoever in,

words for you and yours
no longer found
in anybody's speech or written language.
In office archives the vault
of listings & deeds either lifts great wings
into distances, or else it wilts
into the buckling floors.

All day, little ill
bothers & little good heartens
my nature. I raise
a wet index finger to check, & an evening
breeze, fresh from indulging itself in the intimate
tissues of living things, drops off a bit, & thus

bringeth the cat her unique small kill
to my doorstep, Chicago's three-
day rain not far behind her.
Selfishly may her genes
—rampant for the time being—
devise as they go the muscular, nervous
contraption they drive
(not for her sake)
as long as they possibly can.

PROSPECTOR, WITH GOLD DUST

Addled with sunbursts & helplessly
fixed in a single lizard's look, I
blushed gray, my face grew a bush
of dry blossoms the wind rattled. Day
after day time didn't tell, almost didn't
follow me. I redoubled worth
my weight in sand by now, trudge the bags along.

Donkey love, my plucky, don't
desert me tonight, not with the pickax, not
with the sieve & the thumbed Savior! From town to
town some dance piano already shudders its way: kick up
the first of its keys jolted off in the poor pitted
trail & later the owl wonders
about it weightily, momentarily.

O before riches maddens me & the coddles
baffle my soul & fine art afflicts my joy,
I admire the sidewinder, piece by excellent
piece of work it does. Still, behind each
such creature chaste in its rationale I suspect
the Disheartener lurking, that reels the wanton
conjecture so powerfully out of heaven.

JINX TODAY

Under a tirade of jays &
not without delivering her
evilest hiss the cat backs off who
yesterday carried along her
gartersnake in contortions smartly,
head high not to drag, swift
level predator gait—

flush once, next mortified!
The outwit who wags this world
at us leers & burnishes all afternoon
in my enterprise, too. I conclude
spent half-heartsore on dwindle &
less to make of it, I'm his
chuckle, his day's favorite.

Come nightfall while the cat & I
merely groom at our furs, he sups
on a broth of our mothers and theirs,
dips it at table, nods & departs.
Here, pussens mine, of Tuesday's chop
I'll share you a gristle. O doesn't the wind
itself that would peel away houses whine!

QUICKSILVER

Spillway: I was treading water.
Exertion took me the long
way around, through the seep
in my track, seep in my compass and collar
& duffel, to sleep at a puddle.
Tread water is what the clearing moon
gloss out on the lake does, too.

Dream about it. Go ahead, spatter
my face, I'm a warm mammal. I'm the detective.
Investigate after the bloodhound laps: commotion
in her dish dies down, the water
subsides to fix a tiny moon. Speaking of
my magnifying glass, I noticed at once that the words

could propagate under the circumstances:
rocked yachts half-hitched in their slips
in repercussion opposite.

THE FENNEC

ran up the glass side, swung
down and ran up the glass side opposite.
It did that over and over.
It looked like a fox and had huge ears like wings.

Fox face with wings,
the body delivers world
after world. Even as people think mind
switches around only in certain cells

each revisits a fennec,
tireless, white as the sun.

GREGOR SAMSA

thought too what
they all thought
and came true

prayed to the body
not to obey
him not to express him

begged shape they make me
wear for company
hold

but felt it start
tried to trick it tried
to change his mind

felt it still happen
his life going
on the same one

going to say it all one
way or another and the truth
is everyone will manage

TISSUE

Enemies are hunting it down.
Because it is worlds' flesh, the kinds of it,
threaded through the mindful
spindles at mitosis,
maintain as their own its recourse
to undifferentiate back;

so it quits the human first, next puts trick
after trick off behind it, sheds limbs, skins,
vessels, nerves, organs, drops every link;
evacuates as they close in
priceless inventions to a blown beach
litter of provocative empties.

It wins, it has unevolved, it
cannot be told from the water.
If it had eyes it would
shine hate, if teeth, would snap,
voice, would shriek; if for the need the right
body would mass & swell again, strike.

DOG

Get back you
dog better get
outta here
fast I'll smash your
bad brown eyes, snarly,

you dog,
I got nothin worth
more than breakin it
down your big
fur head,

got tools
can do you up like
brown paper
parcels with
twine,

up lots
of presents & out
to fancy
addresses,
'cause the dogs

out there been
eatin on
me too, you, get a
wise dog's ass
off premises, quick.

BULLY

Bully for you, you made Glee Club.
A trumpet voluntary for you!—
but the Safety Patrol monitor lizard
ruffles around to me when I call.

You made high C, the suicide note.
Attention-getter! —a smattering
stirs the bleachers & I too murmur
up a platitude as it ruffles around to me.

Glee Club folds away scales & keys.
Kitchen fixes everybody microwave
lemonade, especially the membership
convened for the monitor lizard.

A trumpet major's *embouchure,* they say,
excites girls. I play the slither. I chalk up
your sorry excuse for a solo to military
precision, hotshot; absent on remote patrol.

Voluntary for you, but the predatory
mandator, aroused, slides its bracelets in its
locker. I had to compose it this paper song.
Nothing checks it but the safety.

INHUMANE

Monkey lightning cranks
down the rungs of the usual dark
night of the soul. *Strike you, you
wish,* hisses each of several consecutive
sentences, one per each
million-or-so victims, mistaking for me
my alter ego, the punk convict,

even as brilliant electricity,
halowise, fires around the protected,
harmless hairs of his head. I smell you—
ozone edge, sulfur. Frazzled institutional
calendar, picked over, volunteers execution
dates nobody else wants: who rubs
me out every time I pencil myself in?

When did even the crickets quit my yard?
Harsh garden: thieving bunnies, the ones kids
ambush for fun, dispatched in earnest convulsions—
guard, go dig me up a bunch of them!
But lickety-split lasts, lasts,
persists, protracts. Convict, the gifted escapee,
consults the yellow nails of his underhandedness

(may they rise by their moons in spite),
and so he clambers up, bravo!, to rip &
ricochet among the livid silver
linings of perfect crime, a skill,
a skull, a skeleton, *modus operandi* I'd
think to mimic myself, only drop to quadruped:
may the brute force condescend to me.

NOUEMENT

Even as that one girl of extraordinary
early gifts gently embowered the skittish
uncouth unicorn, a lesser earthworm from under
the plinth of the garden urn improved
its own furrow with slick
of their double sweet
bee-spit, honey-
sputter & droopy yellow dust. Yet another
hummingbird's compact body knocked in the air up
underneath particular purples.
                      Caught
in the art-act, girl's petals fastening
eloquently now in the innumerable
ringlets of its blond coat, the shivering imaginary
creature lost its track of proper time, forgot
certain essential meanders along the way
from midsummer to winter range,
& finally, when it did entirely kneel
down & bowed forward into the soft loop she knotted,
it did so to tolerate only
the very name about to occur to her.

WATCH

Dogs in a circle with men know
it will be music
trumpets, whistles, tambourines, the strangest music
to bring them to their feet, but

the first sound is like the clatter of lamb hoofs

the second sound
(as though a wind were
rising in the hangar)
clank of wings

USA DYSPEPTIC

Irritable baby rattle, I hate my name.
I spell like a snake, one letter long.
War twitches magnesium light
on, off, skids the sky, switches sides during the dark
parts when who's whose double *agent*
provocateur forgets, wonders, flutters the two-tongue-
tips where the mnemonic touched once.

Dear human being, permit a spurious
overture, this one, hiss hiss. Either I contrive
or else I waste in a foul mood, your fault.
I wish you your parents' mouthful
of weaponry; once history veers off, a slug
to police your leaf. Drag you useless
legs, magnetic field stinging itself along by inches.

Author of the cartoon fuse, anarch whose lowlife
sizzle nuzzled & snuck the dirt, admired
my gifts & fed me black and red
licorice whips in bed.
Touchy sleeper: I squirm yet, as if to conform to his heel.
Or subside? —confine myself to bouts of angina,
spastic diaphragm, hiccups, the world-

famous burning esophagus? —its taste
the toxic taste two lovers kiss who sipped
each other's sepsis back behind the lush
green verbiage & swapped pet epithets? But I list
under the very alphabet they thumbed.
Maledict! —as diligently as I spittle & slick the latest
civic pretext you unzip, who swallows a word of it?

FREE EXPRESSION ON THE AIRWAVES

Vietnam, 1967

The air discredits the broadcasts.
Incensed homecoming air inverts
weather lidding the people in
with stuff that smells like burnt Asia,
inflames the mucus membranes and
eats away the machinery: bind up the land

Plants' black chimneys like burst bodies
discharge it from helpless insides
Out their holes they issue balloons
like comic things; simple the air
believes them and we will all die
gagging says the honest American big sky

INTERMENT

Insists the right of the left hand, *What were you*
doing yourself those days of plunder,
last days remained to us both? & prods, right index
finger into the left palm,
Wasn't it comparable?—

(scratch I heard from within
the flowery lockbox, stitch in the side
they sew a man up so he won't go bleed
absolutely heartless) —*Un-*
persuaded you add much to a ritual there's not

even otherwise more of, I bet you begged, you
ape-scraped knuckles on the pavement, dinged
a tinny cup, please, sir, moment of your time to time's
ticky two January faces, one wicked & other the one
more-or-less good irrespective its turnabout.

But the left twitches ineptly, merely
electrically, little nerve
lost there. And look! a shady business both
minded shies off too. Childish, who's to pick
& choose? kickup which-over-which greenery clod?

CENTRAL INTELLIGENCE

Believe it! there'll be the odd two, three
dainty birches, for instance— flourishing
enterprises of green spies— airily
totting up any & all of its artless & partial
variants-over-the-years into your final
inexorable confession outright,

dear who; vireos, too, comparing
corroborative notes they'll next
tuck away & off with to the distantly
solicitous authorities they answer to
for their little expectant lives so much
too easily outstripping yours & mine;

& the indiscriminate light
that lies down with anybody,
nestles into anybody's lenient arms,
curls up inside the top
peach & the bottom peach unto the last
basket still picking when the world winks out—

no doubt the least breeze yet to insinuate
among the hairs of your head picks up
your idlest agreeable hum, snatches
of lyric I missed, & sooner or later a name
you'll allow you knew me by, & thereafter bit by bit
the whole shuffle of our poor secrets, my love.

Later & finally, when they zero down to me,
when they send, say, the ocean, bulging with misdemeanor,
to truckle up to my feet on its white knees
so that I must gather it onto my lap, what precious
little then be left & to wheedle after!—a gray pouch
of my baby teeth I want back. Pinch of my birthday dust.

INARTICULATE

Even hereabouts, these days: roving bands
of hungry poems, thuggish, some assaultive by
nine in the morning; all along the palisades

they lurch up from independent
stupors under the rhododendron, beseech
your next-to-last word, some word.

Fussy, though, want a luscious one,
your specialty, split your lip for it. Words!—
& this the lively garbage-ridden barge-

boggling free world fuller
than yesterday, than yester-
moment, even, of ripening-to-the-skies

fair & foul all-weathering language:
everybody ababble on gluts of it & furiously
sweating out the international gagging tongues.

Take a poem home, then, waif one, a girl one, pariah—
nuisance even to her own kind & scuttle;
of wretches you'd notice unlikeliest, never mind

pick to usher in to open up a literate grown
woman's private savories: sweetheart! try *subterfuge;*
bronchial anathema; scourge, growl.

CHAIN LETTER

Send me a modest money & copy
this very verse off ten
times anew for the unlisted
likeminded you might know of & go
ahead, add to it one of your own.
Send all the verses off,
& me the money the ten times.

If you positively recognize
this in advance as one of those tests
you flunk, then copy ten from the lists
of the tests you flunk, add this & send
each off with its modest money
to me care of an institutional
depravity of your choice.

Now you toss helplessly
among contending tens
of your favorites! each one hasn't heard
all these years the least peep
out of you even though you do utter
one many waking moments— time
of day you might've but didn't die,

time of day you brim with gratitude,
flush again for what sweet
houseroom the world makes. Then send
me what time you took to read this
verse this far, if you did; also the blush
making the face in the morning, it
doesn't have to be yours.

3

IN LEVITY

Monarch stopped a minute
on its way to Guatemala, stood & sipt
a clover. Beelzebub, o color &
reticulate my wings, too!

Out of breath, I hurried to catch up
to my body but the wind
buffeted me. Straight out of my erstwhile
element the off-guard flew.

What loops aloft after its prey?
A crab thinks a fish does. A dog
doesn't, it digs. A bat stutters bugs
intelligibly back at itself, but a kite

(fabric, not *Falconidae)* lacks hunger.
Mounting the hill with one knotted on his trout rod
nodded my father, his hunch how to fly it. Maybe
he's turned into a butterfly? Notice me doubt it.

Look how a kite doesn't need! It's a made thing.
It's why the line tugs. *Don't listen to
a word I say* is the one proposition the kite
—as risen ear— diverts & buoys against prayer.

PATERNOSTER

Evening: the ruler settles upon the roost.
All day long we made this much peace. The rest
of the raw material left in the world
keeps for tomorrow.

Wise ruler at peace rests. One eye
of his closes, soon so does the other.
In his dream, as in his amusement, harm
hardly ever befalls but dispels in the air first.

Night in the roost: warm dust
improves its situation upon the breast.
Fresh straw arrived for you. Bricks, bread; so the material
world in absentmindedness governs itself.

Tomorrow the ruler keeps himself
to himself. He has a minor pride to settle
in his better nature: first he inspects his own
bright eye. All day long we make this much peace.

Faint heart! What little malice around the roost
implicates itself in peace. Improvements of mind
keep clique & critic lightly amused. Noon:
I have a matter to govern upon your breast.

Tomorrow settles upon the ruler complete peace.
Doesn't the roost wonder? Mind the absence
of the material world? This much shining day
by day we made. The ancient fresh dust befalling.

UNISON

Who in the rosydawn town blinks
awake fullgrown? Surely each &
every may rise to at least
one such tonic occasion &
likely some several.

Far & away a nerve
plucks that only those certain
citizens' ears catch who know
then to put off all other goods
only barenakedness

& step out so arrayed
into streets themselves revealed
—shining, ardent—
as all one way
to the crisp green common.

We arrive to
unsing the hero, hapless he.
Which note of so many
shall we begin on? Pitchpipe
hum.

DEPARTURE

Stubbed my pencil so I skipped class.
Needn't take notes, copy a graphic,
and as for what day it is it knows without being told.
As soon as I'd never
be missed, I snapped on my slicker.

It looked rainy until I saw straight,
but by then I'd followed the yellow signs
around & around back. Shiny shrubbery
clustered in raked wood chips, sturdy ivy trunks,
nasturtiums, the loudmouth laughable daffodils.

Another thing, I'd like a daddy who'd come back
as one bouffant gray squirrel, though mine wasn't the type.

At dinner, icy butter pats & the very next
morning, from a jet climbing air, the district's entire
fleet of school buses, row upon row in their sorry lot,
but scheduled, I believe,
& then we plunged into the heavy cloud.

MIGRAINE

Displayed under a cold washcloth, mother would moan,
"My head is worse. My head
is worse than a breadbox.
It is worse
than Brussels sprouts, & worse
than the head of God, bulging with wars."
Then God's will despoiled & quit her.

Dangling from a hanging tree her preferred
earrings jittered, tinkled alarm: defamation
incipient somewhere, ignorant, out of turn.
Faintly audible even in her rhinestone egg-
studded bird's
nest brooch recently distributed in my favor, the brawl
she was belle of still rumors on,

albeit too indistinctly now to carry much beyond the bureau.
Crack units, battering blitzes & nauseas that once
mounted to topple her! —but the rear detachments
of misery deteriorate. Seizing merely me, a few
grunts gripe & malinger, kick at my eyes in fits
of chronic demoralization:
nothing left of that brassy dame who grappled the pitiless legions.

VERNAL

Under the world where the
dog digs ardently after only just
one luscious nerve, the dead
brutalize among themselves.
"Here!" hollers the dogmaster, to the dog,
"Fetch that here!"
But the nerves run deeper along to
sweets & knit there & tug hard;
master & dog must make do gnawing at
something else back to home. The dead
too eventually tire of how
tiresome they still are.
Under the world a
mood lightens, a thin
prayer goes praising up to dearest dirt,
croons after roots
in solicitude, bits of flattery, wit,
the whole long story again suggesting
imaginable green.

DEATHTRAP

Hook what you've got of skin & bones in a cut
of yellow fat at the spring pin, & spread both
opposite horizons— jaggedy jaws

firmly down wideopen while an enlarging breeze
distends the stink, & before gloaming darkens
alert Death's nostril has caught it; in blueblack

Death hides its hunch, from every trunk it
snouts out & sidles behind each neighboring
mound & pittipats spotty around the stars,

Death's gone so famished without you yet!
Death's sobbed aloud on its insipid heap for only your
unique salt tang that its glut lacks,

your condiment, your zest, whet of its *oo yes!* last
best appetite. Squat there the night in your own long-
simmering hair, until, just behind wristbeat, when Death

nips, just as you slip your tongue aside
Death's tongue & the trap kicks, shake off your
poor damp paw, negligible, & quit Death gnashing as it

no doubt still will, & hurry, hero! plunge with me
downhill into the clutches of the buttercups, just let
miserable Death yell.

CAPER

Pickpocket Death
eased her out of her one
rosy fold of flesh
in a wink— *who'll know*—

& you know he didn't
need her a bit, nor anyone
else, nor for that
matter covet her even,

no, but he just swipes
in passing, got his one
& twitchy trick so keen to
exercise itself it wheedles

him out of all rest & back
to the business— you remember,
same way the opposite stunt
slicked being from nothing once.

EPIPHANY

One night you watch the snow whirl up; it
quickens in the kitchen window light

old souls & stars
keen aloud for this world,
hurl to be born on this hill,
in the dull barn, out over the black hemlocks.

UNTENABLE

Wet cat, long-haired tail aloft & parted in fronds,
squeezes in doorwise out of the rain, & just so I was born,
slick, quick & slipped (once) through the twice-
in-a-lifetime only

chink-in-things some nicety struck between not-
being & being, to this: ah! —
the ungodly side, where the food is.
Warm bodies here rub the warm body I've got. I'm amazed.

Formerly a null hypothesis (at best, glorified
wild guess), now I occupy premises, keep cats.
Are we not amused? Slightly, almost, unless who's too
brainy today to keep whom company? As if—

mightn't we? —take whim for cue & reciprocate,
gingerly negotiate this instant world unlikelier
than any other, commingling our infinite accidents?
Preposterous coincidence! Gimmick? Intrigue, plot?

Or, yawn, never mind? A lie! Here's mind persistent, mine,
& (once chowed down) all sentience I know transfixed
ahead & scared to death: what next
opens-&-shuts is nix: no-way, the far cry, the forget-it.

RANDOM DIRT ROAD POEM

starts here — look around! not another soul — so it must be you,
mustn't it? off to lose the way this time; shake that
homegoing way, the way underfoot from the outset,

confounded briefly in somebody's dog's company & subject
to such doggy digressions as may vary from moment
to moment hurling recklessly crosswise the obvious.

Presently, whatever dog's long gone. Really, does the world
cry out for narrative? Dear readers riveted in their yards,
heads tipped back, shading their eyes up upon the hired blue

skywriting there? But with any luck you'll disappoint
much of your fortune, miss your compliments to the touchy
old woman— it must be she— who stoops heavily in the ditch

today to set down her dinted pot of gold & clap
for a rainbow, & she'll not, then, riddle your third best guess
with consequence, or press upon you that mousy velvet

wrap of hers with the innermost seam slit. Happily neither
the right fork nor the left fork crazing off from straight ahead
can backtrack yet, nor can the elementary school bus,

stuffed with eyes, raise dust enough to succumb to,
nor, though it putters on methodically, can it effect
any of its stops that the dog that took off before hasn't

dashed around & nosed over thoroughly first for children
(they were dreaming of, or shoving aboard, or squirming hotly
within the bus) & given up, & leapt off. But you've picked

your obliquer way. Rubbing faint cemetery reliefs with a stub
on a scrap, you pause patting yourself down for no pocket
you ever got them out of, or to put them back in now.

Some few headstones beyond, the breeze still vigorously spins
three novelty whirligigs, stuck there since early spring,
paddling out the necessary prayers, probably these:

Tempt no earthly thing but to its gentlest undoing.
Sometimes extricate one or two of our shades from the shade
of trees. Tease subdividing veins out of loose blowy leaves

like those you're chasing after now— no, it was a rubbing!—
past the fenced yard, say, between the next two trailers where the poultry
repartee resumes over whatever it left off being

about, continually beneath notice. They're ducks. Raccoons
quietly snatch through the wire nights & pull the heads right off
their necks & scamper off. But they were only just saying . . .

Also you'll not see the dog again, ever. It's home, fed,
flinches in dreams. In the yard some big bone whistles underground,
from the suck in its marrow, one of those tunes beyond hearing,

& meanwhile, while sooner got later, a weather built; steeply
it clouded up from behind you. Low sun still seeps the last
of its light up through air going pulpy for rain soon,

but the old lady, older now & bitterer with refreshed
disappointment, limps down to the ditch again & fetches
her bright pot back — it never works from twilight to dawn —

& frets: nobody showed up, & she lost a pencil, too,
with the spell it meant to write as she'd guide the little fist
along of some second-grader dropped off out of her district,

& what few blue words showed momentarily visible
overhead against the gray already dissipate: *You're not*
looking where you're going is what they said as you tripped

on less than nothing, on grammar, on some subordinate
clause you were warned about, over and over. *Familiar*
is how things look once you struggle up. Nothing but the highway home.

WHERE IT HURTS

Won't catch a verse of mine staring out its window,
goofing, & nary a soul's best
interest at heart, or drooping a lengthy
ash off its contemplative slow burn— o only subside,
delirious fever!

Dear passerby, trust me.
Allow me to finger & pepper that one
wound you still cherish of ignominy, your Jesus-stab
at the rib, in the very hinge of love,
in the moment you first fell under hammer-and-tongs,
nitwitted with wonder

over your first poem, say, that you'd perfectly
lettered in blue crayon,
when, just then, came & over & over
again comes the school bus, o golden
coach that all too soon too openly hisses & flaps
to engorge itself with the others,

lummoxes of prestige, derision & mayhem careening
the rubbery aisle!
                    As you lurched,
as your peacock-iridescent
stanza flutters & self-destructs
with a vengeance so dinky it cannot but captivate
my regard,

this greeting circulates to croon to you: not
a prayer in the world.

FOUR PENNIES

Baby don't cry:
we'll be mother & father &
day after day
we'll have bread & meat & milk &
oranges & sing songs to
sleep & wake up, you'll see;

every once in a while
we'll say over by heart
the names we know the birds by &
names of stars we know,
& close eyes & close
hands inside the grown hands & go

keep time & follow the words.
Baby don't cry:
this is where we live,
here is where we have our
breakfast & birthday &
red boots & red shoes;

one penny is yours to keep,
one penny is mine to keep,
one more for the story & one
more for the storyteller who
told me to tell you
it comes true.

LUMINARY

Tonight one love
courts in Andromeda.
Stars afloat like the milk
after war stir more than desire,
spread more than treasure or hoard
or than bread:

From little, from light & less,
trim silver planks for the sides & peaks of home,
drive the clean spikes deep in bone,
devise
upon them estate & tinder until
we will dwell there pure
or burn entire.

NOTHING TO BRAG ABOUT

Easy come, who else are you? Easy go, or I misremember:
Mumbo-the-jumbo boy, whose first step forward led
my first step back, that dance.

Mother flowered my hair
florid, a mistake. I'd've rathered bats. Happier
fellow-creature he'd've been too, who won me, prized

up my fingertip grip, we'd've flocked the buggy void
around the athletic field, twister between the eyes
where the blind gland glows inside.

Gymnasium spasm, alas! whispering drums, sneeze
that honked a catching disease over the Prom Queen—
she, too, ruptured, ill-disposed-of by a tiara,

& I myself never did marry once that mattered.
The children mate & wander, whose abandoned rooms
groom their furniture & yearn, whose windows glaze,

& I fix my sling in Pandora, the constellation that rises.
A knotty hammock song serves. Flying trapezes pick up
& drop off spectacular passengers, and the elegant

elephant who laid me end-to-end around the ring
year in & out still wonders what she was born to do.
Great gray ears, it's me, still speaking to you.

PENULTIMATES

for William Matthews

1.

Bee in my bonnet Death
thy sting, lay ye down
hum & hive
into the Black Hole.

2.

Cook dabbles in the stew, observes,
"No such thing as too much parsimony!"

3.

Think how terse the
one Word is.

FETCH

Because I roar & toss, it seemed
to my ear that a dog so-to-spoke
by a deathbed: *Mistress! the ocean*

thuds the stacks from ballyhoo
to conundrum, & out deep it minds
the motherhood of all clutter; fishes

infest the bric-a-brac, even the silt
down, down the awful trench glows,
so I'm off to go snap up foam—

but it was only hell's bells, wasn't it?
& surf on the porch half the night
woof-woofed: *look what the moon,*

all by itself! chased up & left for you, —you,
the shiny one of every single thing to me—
one more of everything.

Acknowledgments

Poems in this collection, some in slightly different form, have appeared elsewhere, as follows:

ACM: "Watch" (part of "Two Merriments")
Alaska Quarterly Review: "St. John's Head, Hoy, Orkney Islands"
American Literary Review: "Chagrin," "Feathered Friends," "Ghazal Y2K" (as "Ghazal 2000"), "Jinx Today"
Anon: "Cohabitation: Mind and Body"
Barrow Street: "Memento Mori"
beyond baroque: "Gregor Samsa," "Watch"
Boston Review: "Central Intelligence" (as "Intelligence"), "Chain Letter," "The Particulars" (reprint)
Colorado Review: "Invocation"
Columbia: "Caper"
Confluence: "Indicative," "Quicksilver," "Resurgent"
Cotyledon: "Penultimates"
CutBank: "Vernal"
DeKalb Literary Arts Journal: "Zodiac" (as "For the Twelve Houses")
Epoch: "Incarnation," "The Particulars"
Field: Contemporary Poetry and Poetics: "Mistress Here," "Where It Hurts"
Georgetown Review: "Tissue"
The Gettysburg Review: "Migraine"
Hunger Mountain: "Departure"
Indiana Review: "Sentimental"
The Iowa Review: "Introductory"
The Journal: "In Levity"
The Kenyon Review: "Hypnagogic"
Manoa: "Deathtrap," "Epiphany"
The Marlboro Review: "Away/Home," "Punctual"
the minnesota review: "The Fennec"
New Orleans Review: "Inhumane," "Prospector, with Gold Dust"
Nimrod: "Chatter," "The Two Bowls"
Northwest Review: "Fetch," "Hysteria," "Lapis," "Nouement," "Random Dirt Road Poem," "Reverberant," "Tomato Aspic Elegy," "Unison"
Notre Dame Review: "Counter-Fable," "Interment," "Nothing to Brag About"
The Ohio Review: "Getting Away"
Oxford Magazine: "Veronica"
Pequod: "Bubblebath," "Urogenital," "USA Dyspeptic"

Perihelion (online): "Brainwash," "Green Velvet," "Luminary," "Midsummer Marital, with Creosote Bush & Tattoo," "Paternoster," "Untenable"

Ploughshares: "Bully"

Poetry Daily (online): "Sentimental" (reprint)

Prairie Schooner: "The Highest Standard of Living in the World," "We May All Know"

The Progressive: "Agley"

Sojourners: "Four Pennies"

Soundings: "Free Expression on the Airwaves"

Sou'wester: "Palaver," "Witnesses"

Stand Magazine (U.K.): "Quintessa"

Verse Daily (onli ne): "Lapis" (reprint), "Reverberant" (reprint)

Willow Springs: "Atmospherics," "Facetious"

The Vermont Arts Council published the author's chapbook, *Powers,* which included "Dog," "Gregor Samsa" and "Out"; "Ghazal: Intervals" was included in Agha Shahid Ali's anthology, *Ravishing DisUnities: Real Ghazals in English* (Wesleyan University Press, 2000); Stigworm.com/worms, a website devoted to worms, ran "Agley" as a "crawl" along the bottom of its pages for a while.

I thank: The University of Michigan, for Avery Hopwood and Jule Hopwood Awards for a manuscript including "Cohabitation: Mind and Body"; The Vermont Studio Center; Agha Shahid Ali, Reginald Gibbons, Tom Lux, Heather McHugh, Steve Orlen, and the Warren Wilson College Master of Fine Arts Program for Writers; and Nancy Krim, Greg Rappleye, and, especially, Muriel Nelson.

Other books from Tupelo Press:

This Nest, Swift Passerine, Dan Beachy-Quick
Cloisters, Kristin Bock
Stone Lyre: Poems of René Char,
   translated by Nancy Naomi Carlson
Psalm, Carol Ann Davis
Orpheus on the Red Line, Theodore Deppe
Spill, Michael Chitwood
staring at the animal, John Cross
Then, Something, Patricia Fargnoli
Calendars, Annie Finch
Other Fugitives & Other Strangers, Rigoberto González
Keep This Forever, Mark Halliday
Inflorescence, Sarah Hannah
The Us, Joan Houlihan
Red Summer, Amaud Jamaul Johnson
Dancing in Odessa, Ilya Kaminsky
Ardor, Karen An-hwei Lee
Dismal Rock, Davis McCombs
Biogeography, Sandra Meek
Flinch of Song, Jennifer Militello
At the Drive-In Volcano, Aimee Nezhukumatathil
The Beginning of the Fields, Angela Shaw
Selected Poems, 1970–2005, Floyd Skloot
Nude in Winter, Francine Sterle
Embryos & Idiots, Larissa Szporluk
Archicembalo, G.C. Waldrep
The Book of Whispering in the Projection Booth,
   Joshua Marie Wilkinson
Narcissus, Cecilia Woloch
American Linden, Matthew Zapruder

See our complete backlist at www.tupelopress.org